# The Divine Order of Faith

By
Pastor Creflo A. Dollar Jr.

If you would like more information about this ministry, or are interested in becoming a partner, please write:
WORLD CHANGERS MINISTRIES
Post Office Box 490124
College Park, Georgia 30349

Editorial and Creative services provided by:
Vision Communications
169 E. 32nd
Edmond, OK 73013
(405) 348-7995

Cover design by:
Virgil Lynn Design
405-348-7965

Unless otherwise indicated, all Scripture quotations are from the KING JAMES VERSION.

AMP – Amplified Version
NIV – New International Version

**The Divine Order of Faith**
ISBN: 0-9634781-1-7

# Table of Contents

## Dedication

This book is lovingly dedicated to
Pastor Chester L. Carter, Sr. and
Sister Laura Carter—my pastors, teachers
and friends. Your Christ-like example,
wise counsel and innumerable prayers
have made all the difference
in this ministry.
Bless you.

# Chapter 1
# Is Your Faith Out of Order?

**Let all things be done decently and in order.**
**(I Corinthians 14:40)**

Frustration. I see it on the faces of many believers who tell me they just can't seem to get "this faith stuff" to work for them.

I can sympathize. Early in my Christian life, I too spent a lot of time scratching my head and wondering why I wasn't seeing the miracles I needed so desperately.

Now I know. The key to seeing miracle-working power operate consistently in your life lies in understanding the divine order of faith.

When I talk about "divine order," I'm referring to the fact that God has ordained everything in heaven and on earth to operate according to a predetermined sequence or order.

This is especially true where spiritual things are concerned. God's heavenly kingdom is a place of order.

For example, under the Old Covenant system, the High Priest followed a very strict, very detailed sequence of actions before he dared to enter the Holy of Holies.

He didn't go waltzing into the Most Holy Place any time he pleased. I assure you, he would have only done so once. Such a cavalier attitude toward God's prescribed order would have cost him his life.

No. There was a process that had to take place before the High Priest could operate in certain aspects of his calling. The same is true for you and me where faith is concerned.

You'll never see the miracles and promises of God that will move you from the problem to the solution until you come to understand the divine order of faith.

## Follow the Procedure

Even in everyday life, there is an established order to follow in much of what we do. And as the pastor of a large and growing congregation, I frequently see people who fail to follow the set order.

From time to time, for example, an irate church member will come up to me and say, "Pastor, I've been trying to get in to see you for five months!"

Then I ask them how they've gone about trying to see me.

"Well, I've dropped by your office several times and you're either gone, busy, or have someone in your office."

Immediately the problem is evident. There is a simple and well established procedure in our church for getting in to see the pastor. It is spelled out clearly in our new member orientation.

Anyone who wants to see me merely needs to call my secretary, get an appointment, and show up on the day and time set. That's all there is to it.

I have established a clear order for arranging my office schedule. If you don't follow the order, you probably don't get in to see me.

The same is true in the Kingdom of God. The Lord has a set order for everything. As we see in I Corinthians 14, that includes the exercise of the gifts of the Spirit:

> **If any man speak in an unknown tongue, let it be by two, or at the most by three, and that by course; and let one interpret. But if there be no interpreter, let him keep silence in the church; and let him speak to himself, and to God. Let the prophets speak two or three, and let the other judge. If any thing be revealed to another that sitteth by, let the first hold his peace. For ye may all prophesy one by one, that all may learn, and all may be comforted. And the spirits of the prophets are subject to the prophets. For God is not the author of confusion, but of peace, as in all churches of the saints. Let all**

**things be done decently and in order. (I Corinthians 14:27-33,40)**

I've been in situations where God's prescribed order for operating in the gifts of the Spirit was ignored.

One person would jump up and give a message in tongues, and before anyone could give an interpretation, someone else would be up doing the same thing.

Soon there were people all over the place delivering some type of prophetic message. The result was total chaos, and no one was getting blessed.

## No Order, No Miracles

When you neglect God's divine order, His blessings don't flow. Divine order is a prerequisite for miracles and blessings.

We see that truth illustrated so vividly in Jesus' feeding of the 5,000. Before the people could be miraculously blessed, they had to get in order.

**For they were about five thousand men. And he said to his disciples, Make them sit down by fifties in a company. (Luke 9:14)**

Can you imagine the chaos that would have ensued if the disciples had started randomly handing out food to that hungry mob? There would have been a riot!

There's no getting around it. Follow God's set order and you'll get the desired results. Ignore it and you'll end up frustrated and defeated.

So does God have an established order when it comes to overcoming problems? Yes. The scriptures give us a clear pattern for moving from any problem—be it sickness, debt, lack, family strife or anything else—to the solution.

These steps will work for anyone at any time, regardless of how overwhelming the circumstances you face. These steps represent God's divine order of faith.

We've had a lot of good teaching on faith. But I've heard very little on God's prescribed order for using it. I believe that's why we have so many so-called faith failures out there and so many frustrated Christians. Most don't even know there is a divine order of faith, much less understand what it is.

In the following pages we'll see that God's Word lays out a simple 10 step order for getting from any problem to a miraculous solution. It doesn't matter if you've been a Christian for 50 years or you were born again 5 minutes ago. If you will submit yourself to this order, your faith will produce. God's Word guarantees it.

But before you can submit to God's divine order for faith, you need to have a good working understanding of what faith is.

# Chapter 2
# You Gotta Have Faith

**The just shall live by faith. (Romans 1:17)**

We are living in extraordinary times. Signs all around us shout the fact that we are living in the final days of history. And in this critical hour, knowing how to operate in faith can literally mean the difference between life and death.

That's why it is vital you start developing your faith now. If you wait until a crisis is upon you to start learning how to live by faith, you'll be in big trouble. Those who put it off until the last minute will find that it's too late.

Child of God, the time for playing church is over. The King of Kings and the Lord of Lords is on His way back. And the key to surviving and even thriving in this unprecedented era is knowing how to operate in faith.

## No Avoiding Trouble

Regardless of the time in history in which you're living, if you're a believer, one thing is certain. You're going to have trouble. It's not only likely. It's guaranteed. In John 16:33 Jesus says,

> **These things I have spoken unto you, that in me ye might have peace. In the world ye shall have tribulation: but be of good cheer; I have overcome the world.**

It shouldn't come as any great shock when, as a believer, you experience tribulation or trouble. Jesus said it would happen. But praise God, that's not all He said.

Jesus went on to say, "Cheer up! I have overcome the world!"

Now the world hasn't changed all that much since Jesus' day. Sure, the technology has advanced, but human nature is as mean and nasty as ever. Without Jesus, this world is a hostile place.

Yet Jesus tells us to be of good cheer because He has overcome. But knowing that really doesn't help all that much unless He also tells us how He overcame, so we can do the same.

We need to know what it takes to overcome poverty and lack, what we can do to overcome certain destructive habits, and what is needed to enable us to overcome sickness. In other words, "Don't just tell me you overcame; Tell me how I can do it, too!"

In I John 5:4 that's precisely what Jesus does.

> **For whatsoever is born of God overcometh the world: and this is the victory that overcometh the world, even our faith.**

There it is. The first prerequisite for overcoming the world is being "born of God." There's no use even trying to be a world overcomer if you're not born again.

The second part of that verse tells us what enables us to overcome—our faith. Jesus overcame the world by using His faith and we'll do it the same way.

Faith is the key. It hasn't passed away. It's not something out of a dusty old sermon. Faith is fresh, alive, powerful and more relevant today than at any time in history. And if you're going to overcome the world rather than being overcome by it, you're going to do it with your faith.

Too many people in the church today are trying to overcome their problems with pop psychology, government programs or something they read in a magazine somewhere.

The truth is, you can't separate victory from faith. To experience one you have to have the other.

### Live It

God is serious about His people operating in faith. In fact, four separate times in the Scripture, God declares,

"The just shall live by faith" (Habakkuk 2:4, Romans 1:17, Galatians 3:11, Hebrews 10:38).

Now, the Bible says, "in the mouths of two or three witnesses shall every word be established" (Matthew 18:16, II Corinthians 13:1). Yet here is the testimony of four voices proclaiming the same thing. Do you get the impression God wants us to live by faith?

"Brother Dollar, I tried that faith thing and it didn't work." Well, it didn't say, "the just shall try it out." It said, "the just shall live by faith." You don't dabble in faith. You live it.

Who are the just? Anyone who's a born-again child of God. When Jesus washes your sins away you are declared righteous by God Himself. If you're saved, you're one of the "just." And as one of the just, you must learn to live by faith.

## So What Is It?

Once you understand that trouble is inevitable, and faith is the only thing that will overcome that trouble, the next step is to find out what this thing called faith really is.

You may be thinking, "Everybody knows what faith is. It means belief or trust."

Of course, that's part of it. But real faith involves so much more than that. And any biblical discussion of the nature of faith has to start with Hebrews chapter 11:

> **Now faith is the substance of things hoped for, the evidence of things not seen. For by it the elders obtained a good report. Through faith we understand that the worlds were framed by the word of God, so that things which are seen were not made of things which do appear. By faith Abel offered unto God a more excellent sacrifice than Cain, by which he obtained witness that he was righteous, God testifying of his gifts: and by it he being dead yet speaketh. By faith Enoch was translated that he should not see death; and was not found, because God had trans-**

**lated him: for before his translation he had this testimony, that he pleased God. But without faith it is impossible to please him: for he that cometh to God must believe that he is, and that he is a rewarder of them that diligently seek him. (Hebrews 11:1-6)**

Notice the first word of the first verse. "Now faith is..."

The first thing you need to understand is faith operates in the realm of the now. God is not yesterday. God is not tomorrow. God abides in the eternal now. He didn't tell Moses His name was "I WAS." He called Himself "I AM."

That's good news, because when you're sick, God says, "I AM your healer." When you need finances, He says, "I AM your provider." When you're in trouble, you don't need deliverance someday. You need it now.

The next remarkable thing these verses teach us about faith is that it is a "substance." "Faith is the substance of things hoped for..." In other words, faith is a literal, unseen material. It is "stuff."

The next verse tells us faith is the agency through which the physical universe was made.

**Through faith we understand that the worlds were framed by the word of God, so that things which are seen were not made of things which do appear. (Hebrews 11:3)**

Think of it. Everything you see around you is the product of faith-filled words. Think of God's words as spiritual seeds—seeds that have the ability to produce material, physical things like trees, planets or money.

That's why the Bible is such an enormously powerful thing. From cover to cover it contains God's faith-filled words, specifically empowered to produce whatever you need in your life.

When you pick up your Bible, you hold in your hands the seeds to produce finances, healing, salvation of your loved ones, a sound mind, restoration of your marriage, or anything else you could possibly need.

The tragic fact is that many believers are simply too lazy to get the seed out and plant it. Successful farming takes some effort. And far too many of us want spiritual welfare. We want to line up in a prayer line for a handout, but it doesn't work that way.

A farmer's seed does him no good as long as it lies dormant in the sack. But when he plants, he gets a harvest. Likewise, the seeds of provision in God's Word will never produce for you as long as your Bible gathers dust on your shelf.

"But Pastor Dollar, what if I don't know how to plant the seed of God's Word?" That's what this book is all about. As I said in the opening chapter, there is a specific divine order for getting from the problem to the answer. To find out what that order is, read on.

# Chapter 3
# Step One: Identify the Problem

**In the world ye shall have tribulation: but be of good cheer; I have overcome the world.**
**(John 16:33)**

Before you can expect to get from the problem to the answer, you must first clearly define and understand the exact nature of the problem you're facing. Is it spiritual? Physical? Emotional? Financial? Whatever it is, the first step in conquering it is facing it head on and identifying what it truly is.

That may seem to be a pretty obvious place to start, but you'd be surprised how many believers launch out in search of a solution to a problem they haven't really pinpointed.

Make no mistake about it—problems are going to come. As we saw in the previous chapter, Jesus said we can bank on it. "In this world ye shall have tribulation..."

In Philippians 3:10, Paul sheds additional light on the issue:

> **That I may know him [Christ], and the power of his resurrection, and the fellowship of his sufferings, being made conformable unto his death...**

What does it mean to "know...the fellowship" of Jesus' sufferings? Probably not what you think. This verse isn't telling you to be prepared to be a loser for Jesus. Quite the opposite, actually.

First of all, the Greek word translated "sufferings" here means "to bear up under" or "to withstand." In other words, Paul is saying he wants to know how to hold up under adverse circumstances, not how to gracefully surrender to them.

Jesus was an overcomer. He obtained absolute victory in every trial, temptation and test He ever faced. Therefore, when you enter into the fellowship of His sufferings, you can take anything the devil throws at you and even toss it right back in his face. So, how do you do that?

There is only one way you are going to truly be a partaker in Jesus' victory, and that's through the Word. The seeds of victory over any circumstance you may ever face are in the Word right now. But be prepared. The devil doesn't take kindly to you digging into the source of his defeat.

### Two Sources of Trouble

One of the first things you'll notice when you start getting serious about getting God's Word into your heart and mind is an increase in problems. That surprises a lot of believers.

"But Pastor Dollar, "I thought diving into the Bible was going to quickly solve all my problems!" If that's what you think, child of God, you're mistaken.

What the Word does is give you the power to overcome any problem. And as we learn from Jesus in the parable of the sower, Satan's number one objective is to steal that Word from your heart. If he can't do that, he'll use problems to try to choke it out:

> **The sower soweth the word. And these are they by the way side, where the word is sown; but when they have heard, Satan cometh immediately, and taketh away the word that was sown in their hearts. And these are they likewise which are sown on stony ground; who, when they have heard the word, immediately receive it with gladness; And have no root in themselves, and so endure but for a time: afterward, when affliction or persecution ariseth for the word's sake, immediately they are offended. (Mark 4:14-17)**

Notice that first phrase. "The sower soweth the word." We saw in the previous chapter that the Bible contains seeds of answers for every problem you face.

Then Jesus said, "And these are they by the way side, where the word is sown; but when they have heard..." Hearing the Word is vitally important. If Satan can stop you from hearing the Word concerning a certain subject, he's on his way to defeating you in that area of your life.

"...but when they have heard, Satan cometh immediately, and taketh away the word that was sown in their hearts." Who comes? Satan. When does he come? Immediately.

As long as you ignore God's Word, you're no threat to Satan. But when you start planting God's Word in your heart, he flies into action. He simply can't permit you to put the awesome creative forces of faith-filled words to work in your life. It will undo everything the devil has been working for where you're concerned.

If he fails in stealing the Word from your heart as soon as you receive it, the devil's next ploy will be to come at you with trouble and cause you to be offended at God. Remember Jesus' parable: "...when they have heard the word, immediately receive it with gladness; And have no root in themselves, and so endure but for a time: afterward, when affliction or persecution ariseth for the word's sake, immediately they are offended."

This represents one of the two main sources of problems in any believer's life. Trials, persecution, affliction and trouble all can come as Satan desperately tries to keep God's Word from doing its work in your heart.

### Self-Inflicted Wounds

We've seen how problems can come as Satan tries to choke out the seed of the Word in your life. The other way trouble can enter is through the bad seed you plant yourself. Look at I Peter 2:20:

**For what glory is it, if, when ye be buffeted for your faults, ye shall take it patiently?**

And I Peter 4:15:

**But let none of you suffer as a murderer, or as a thief, or as an evildoer, or as a busybody in other men's matters.**

These verses tell us many Christians suffer, not because of an attack of the devil, but because of their own actions. Sins, evil words, and unrighteous attitudes can all result in an increase in trouble.

I recall hearing about a young lady who was complaining about constantly being approached by rude and offensive men. She was binding the devil and wondering why she wasn't seeing any results. Then someone pointed out that she tended to wear dresses that looked like they were painted on.

She was dressing like a loose woman and acting shocked that men were treating her like one. In reality, she was simply reaping a harvest of bad seeds she had sown.

### Be a Judge

The first step in God's divine order of faith is identifying the source and nature of the problem you are facing. That requires you to become a good judge.

As you prepare to attack a problem with the weapon of faith, examine that problem carefully. First, determine its source. Is it a result of past sins or mistakes? If so, repent and make restitution if appropriate.

Is it the result of the devil trying to drive the Word of God from your heart? If so, get a specific feel for the root of the problem. It may be sickness, fear, family strife, financial lack or any number of other troubles. Once you know precisely what your problem is and where it's coming from, you're ready to take the next step in God's divine order of faith.

# Chapter 4
# Step Two: The Quality Decision

**Multitudes, multitudes in the valley of decision: for the day of the LORD is near in the valley of decision. (Joel 3:14)**

Once you have a handle on what the problem is, the next step is to make a quality decision to overcome it by faith. In other words, choose.

The ability to choose, our free moral agency, is one of the main ways in which we're made in the image of God. Every person born into the earth has a God-given capacity and right to choose.

Furthermore, we're born into a world where everything operates by decision. This is especially true where spiritual things are concerned. In reality, Christianity is really nothing more than a series of decisions.

For example, Jesus died on the cross so that you might have forgiveness of sins and inherit eternal life. But that fact does you absolutely no good unless you make a decision to receive what He did for you. God is honor-bound to respect and protect your right to choose. Even if that means letting you spend eternity in hell, if you choose to do so.

You can say, "I'm waiting on God." But God is saying, "No, I'm waiting on you. Decide." He can't move until you make a decision on which way you're going to go. Life or death, the choice is yours. Deuteronomy 30:19 says so:

> **I have set before you life and death, blessing and cursing: therefore choose life, that both thou and thy seed may live.**

The preeminence of man's right to choose is a theme you'll see repeated throughout the entire Bible. Truly, we all live in "the valley of decision."

## Man the Chooser

How much does God's Word have to say about the power of your choices? A lot. From Genesis to Revelation you'll find the Scriptures emphasizing different aspects of Man's decision-making power. Let's look at just a few:

**And if it seem evil unto you to serve the LORD, choose you this day whom ye will serve; whether the gods which your fathers served that were on the other side of the flood, or the gods of the Amorites, in whose land ye dwell: but as for me and my house, we will serve the LORD. (Joshua 24:15)**

**Go and say unto David, Thus saith the LORD, I offer thee three things; choose thee one of them, that I may do it unto thee. (II Samuel 24:12)**

A change in status, whether good or bad, always begins with a decision. Whatever direction you're moving, it's a result of past choices.

**Let us choose to us judgment: let us know among ourselves what is good. (Job 34:4)**

**What man is he that feareth the LORD? him shall he teach in the way that he shall choose. (Psalm 25:12)**

**For that they hated knowledge, and did not choose the fear of the LORD: (Proverbs 1:29)**

**Envy thou not the oppressor, and choose none of his ways. (Proverbs 3:31)**

Are you facing a seemingly enormous problem? No amount of prayer, no amount of counselling, nothing will make your situation better until you make a choice. All the spiritual activity in the world won't make a bit of difference if you haven't first decided to do things God's way.

**Butter and honey shall he eat, that he may know to refuse the evil, and choose the good. (Isaiah 7:15)**

**For thus saith the LORD unto the eunuchs that keep my sabbaths, and choose the things that please me, and take hold of my covenant... (Isaiah 56:4)**

**Choosing rather to suffer affliction with the people of God, than to enjoy the pleasures of sin for a season... (Hebrews 11:25)**

**I have chosen the way of truth: thy judgments have I laid before me. (Psalm 119:30)**

## A Quality Decision

Faith's power to change your circumstances is not going to operate in your life until you *decide* you are going to live by faith. This requires what I call a "quality decision."

A quality decision is one on which you're willing to stake your very life. It's not an "ought to" decision. It's not a "probably" decision. It's a determined, resolved "I will" decision.

Why is such a firm exercise of your will so important? Because when you're trying to move from your problem to your answer, "decision" is the door. Nobody moves into the reality of God's answers without passing through the door of decision. Decision is the open door into reality.

Waiting on the other side of that door is Almighty God—ready and willing to back you up with all of heaven's power. God will move earth and sky on behalf of someone who has purposed to do things by the book. You make the decision—God will back you up.

Until you walk through the door of decision, God cannot and will not do a thing for you. You have to get fed up with where you are. You have to tear the devil's yoke of bondage off your neck and throw it down. All of heaven is waiting on your decision of quality.

Are you going to choose to continue to live with that problem and let it defeat you, or are you going to make a firm, unwavering decision to overcome it?

This is an essential step in the divine order of faith and it's precisely where many people miss it. They're half-hearted or wishy-washy in their commitment to win.

This wimpy sort of resolve will never move you to the place of victory.

You've got to say, "I'm coming out of this situation. I'm coming out by the power of God and I'm coming out by the Word. I've made my decision and from this point forward, nothing is going to change my mind."

When you've made that kind of quality decision, then, and only then, are you ready to move on to the next step in God's divine order.

# Chapter 5
# Step Three: Finding Your "Title Deed"

**Now faith is the evidence of things hoped for...**
**(Hebrews 11:1)**

Evidence. Our entire system of justice is based on it. For example, when a district attorney brings you into court to accuse you of a crime, he'd better have some convincing evidence to support his claim. He must produce fingerprints, witnesses or some other type of testimony. Otherwise, the judge is going to throw the case out of court and have a stern talk with that D.A.!

The same can be said of your faith in the spiritual court of heaven. If you're going to claim that healing, provision, peace, safety or some other spiritual blessing belongs to you, you'd better have some evidence to back it up.

The fact is, most of the time when Christians pray and "believe" for such things, they come to heaven's court without a shred of evidence to substantiate their claims. As a result, the devil and his crew just laugh and continue to commit their crimes.

This brings us to the third step in God's divine order of faith. Once you've determined in your heart that you're going to overcome by the Word of God, the next step is to go to God's Word and find a promise that speaks to your particular situation. That promise is your legal evidence and your "title deed" to the power and provision of Almighty God.

## Find Your Evidence

**Now faith is the substance of things hoped for, the evidence of things not seen. For by it the elders obtained a good report. Through faith we understand**

**that the worlds were framed by the word of God, so that things which are seen were not made of things which do appear. (Hebrews 11:1-3)**

In a previous chapter we talked about faith being a literal substance—something which is a very real spiritual material. Now let's look at the second part of that phrase. Faith is also..."the evidence of *things* not seen."

Notice that faith is the "evidence of things." Most of the time when you are praying, you are asking and believing for a certain "thing." That *thing* might be money to pay your bills. It might be a new or better car. The *thing* you need could be healing. Whatever it is, faith is the evidence of it. You are not going to obtain any *thing* without faith evidence.

Notice further that faith is the evidence of "things *not seen.*" That's one of the aspects that makes faith seem like such "foolishness" to the natural mind (I Corinthians 2:14). The unrenewed mind says, "Seeing is believing." Or, "I'll believe it when I see it." But real, Bible faith is the believer's evidence that a thing is his, even though he's never seen it!

The Amplified Bible's translation of these verses sheds further light on this important truth.

**Now, faith is the assurance (the confirmation, the title-deed) of the things [we] hope for, being the proof of things [we] do not see and the conviction of their reality—faith perceiving as real fact what is not revealed to the senses. (Hebrews 11:1 AMP)**

That word "confirmation" is instructive. Have you ever called to reserve a rental car? You might call the rent-a-car company and say "I want a black Lincoln Town Car next Tuesday." At that point they would say, "Okay, let me give you a confirmation number."

That confirmation number is your assurance that a black Lincoln has been set aside for your use. Can you see the car? Of course not. Then how do you know you have one? Because that confirmation number is your evidence of a thing not seen.

Should you show up at the rent-a-car counter on the appointed day and be told, "I'm sorry, we don't have a car for you." You can say, "Hold on just a minute! I've got confirmation. Get me a black Town Car now!"

If I showed you the deed to my house, you wouldn't question for a moment that there really was a house at that address. You can't see the house, but my title deed is ample proof that it exists and it is mine.

Child of God, that's the very thing Hebrews 11:1 is trying to communicate to you. If you've been told you have cancer, you can go to the Word and find "By His stripes you were healed." That's your confirmation number, your title deed to health and healing.

Then, when the doctors say you've got three weeks to live, you can hold up your title deed and say with confidence, "I will live and not die because I'm healed by the stripes of Jesus!" You have the proof, the evidence, of your healing. And every devil in hell has to acknowledge and defer to the strength of your evidence.

If you're in a situation where your bills need to be paid and collectors are calling, you can stand up and say, "Hold it! I'm a tither and a giver and Philippians 4:19 says my God shall supply all my needs according to His riches in glory by Christ Jesus."

No matter what you need, regardless of how serious your circumstances, if you will hold on to that title deed, it will surely come to pass. The power of that kind of faith never, never, never fails.

### Be a Detective

How do district attorneys obtain the evidence they present in court? They depend on detectives who snoop and search until they find what they're looking for.

You'll have to do the same thing if you're going to win your case against the devil and everything he's trying to do to you and your family. You're going to have to get out your Bible and search out the verses that speak directly to your particular situation.

I've had sincere people tell me they are believing God for a miraculous healing. When I ask them what they are basing their faith on, they say, "I'm standing on the Word."

"Yes, but what part of the Word?"

"Oh, no part in particular. Just the Word in general."

The Word "in general" won't bring your miracle. Your case will be thrown out for lack of evidence. You need specific evidence from the Bible to bring faith's power onto the scene. And it's entirely up to you to find it. No one else can do it for you.

II Timothy 2:15 says, "Study to shew thyself approved unto God, a workman that needeth not to be ashamed, rightly dividing the word of truth."

There's the key. Study, study, study, study! Of course it's not easy. It calls for a commitment of time and concentration. But it's the only way you're ever going to get the evidence you need to win your case.

Why is finding scriptures that speak to your situation so effective? Because when you locate a Bible verse that promises the thing you need, it energizes your prayer with confidence. I John 5:14,15 says it this way:

> **And this is the confidence that we have in him, that, if we ask any thing according to his will, he heareth us: And if we know that he hear us, whatsoever we ask, we know that we have the petitions that we desired of him.**

Notice it didn't say, "we know we're *going to have* the petitions we desire." It didn't say *someday* we'll have it. It said, "...when we ask...we know that we have the petitions we desired of him." That's present tense...now.

God's Word is His will. His will is His Word. If you see it in your Bible, you can know that it's the expressed, perfect will of God for your life.

If you're new to the Bible and don't know how to find specific promises, get a good concordance. It will give you a list of scriptures for every subject you can imagine.

Once you've found your title deed in God's Word, you can pray and consider the matter settled. In fact, you should start acting as if you possess the thing you've prayed for, because you do!

## Doing It by the Book

You can't dabble in the Word and expect to get results. You can't just "try it out" for a while to see if it will work. Effective faith demands a lifestyle in which you abandon yourself to the Bible. It's an all out commitment to live by the Word, to think by the Word and to talk by the Word.

You see this type of resolve in the most successful people in the Bible:

**...Be it according to thy word... (Exodus 8:10)**

**...Israel did according to the word... (Exodus 12:35)**

**...the children of Levi did according to the word... (Exodus 32:28)**

**...Israel did according to the word... (Exodus 39:32)**

**According to all the Lord commanded... (Exodus 39:42)**

**I have pardoned according to thy word... (Numbers 14:20)**

**...according to all thy commandments... (Deuteronomy 26:13)**

**According to the word of the LORD they gave him the city... (Joshua 19:50)**

**They hearkened therefore to the word of the LORD, (1 King 12:24)**

**...taking heed according to thy word... (Psalm 119:9)**

**...be it unto me according to thy word. (Luke 1:38)**

Whatever you do, make sure you do it according to the Word. It's your evidence and title deed to everything you need.

### Hold on to Your Evidence

Once you've found your title deed, hold on with bulldog tenacity and don't let go.

At first it may seem like nothing is happening. In fact, your outward circumstances may even get worse. No matter what happens, don't let go of your evidence. The writer of Hebrews put it this way:

> **Cast not away therefore your confidence, which hath great recompence of reward. (Hebrews 10:35)**

I don't care how hard it gets; no matter how grim your circumstances appear—regardless of what the doctors, bankers, or neighbors say—hold on to that title deed. God knows how to come through for you right on time.

Child of God, if you're sick, get the evidence of your healing from God's Word. If you're lacking finances, get your evidence. In bondage to habits, get your evidence. Depressed, get your evidence.

No matter what you're facing today, there is a promise in God's Word that addresses your need. A promise you can stake your very life on. Find it, then get ready to move on to the next step in God's divine order.

# Chapter 6
# Step Four:
# Hearing, Hearing, Hearing

**Hear, O my son, and receive my sayings...**
**(Proverbs 4:10)**

So far, you've been given the first three steps of the supernatural sequence that will move you from any problem or crisis to a miraculous solution. They are: (1) Identify the problem, (2) Make a quality decision to overcome the problem, and (3) Find your title deed to an answer in God's Word.

The next link in this chain of victory involves understanding the importance of *hearing* God's Word.

It is difficult to overstate how vital a role hearing plays in your spiritual life. Your ears are one of only two natural gateways to your spirit. Your eyes are the other. And as far as the things of God are concerned, there is no receiving without hearing.

A quick reading of Revelation chapters two and three will illustrate just how serious Jesus is about our hearing His words. Seven different times in two chapters He says:

> **He that hath an ear, let him hear what the Spirit saith unto the churches... (Revelation 2:7, 11, 17, 29; 3:6, 13, 22)**

I'd say the Lord thinks it's important for us to hear what He has to say, wouldn't you?

### The Act of Hearing

Hearing is nothing more than receiving through the "ear gate." However, the Bible kind of hearing involves more than mere listening. It requires attentiveness, belief, and obedience, too. For example, Proverbs 4:10 ties *hearing* directly to *receiving*.

**Hear, O my son, and receive my sayings; and the years of thy life shall be many. (Proverbs 4:10)**

See how the promise of a long, good life is for those who both hear and receive God's wise sayings. "Receive" is another way of saying "obey." If you're not determined to obey what God has spoken, you haven't really received it. James tells us to be: "doers of the word, and not hearers only..." (James 1:22).

Notice that in this verse, the ultimate result of hearing and receiving is long life. At the end of hearing and receiving, there is always a harvest. It's an unstoppable spiritual progression. Hear! Receive! Harvest!

Proverbs 8:34 gives us another view of this truth:

**Blessed is the man that heareth me, watching daily at my gates, waiting at the posts of my doors.**

Blessing is always a result of true hearing. To be blessed means "empowered to prosper." And genuine Bible prosperity deals with much more than money. It involves abundance, peace, and increase in every area of human existence.

In a very real sense, prosperity is the power to control your circumstances instead of your circumstances controlling you. Hearing the Word of God gives you that kind of power.

In other words, the things to which you give your ears determine whether or not you will be able to control a devilish situation directed toward you by the forces of hell.

When Satan tries to put sickness on you and whispers, "You're going to die," having continually heard the Word of healing empowers you to take control of that situation, driving the devil and his lying symptoms out.

If, on the other hand, you've been spending your time listening to the doctor's bad reports, and your relative's stories about all the people they know who died of what you have, you might as well get your affairs in order. You're not empowered to take control of anything.

## Subtle Sounds

I remember the day I got a vivid lesson on the subtle power of what we hear.

Another pastor and I were enjoying a great time of fellowship in a local pizza parlor. We were talking about the Word and the goodness of God. We sat there for several hours, completely caught up in talking about the things of the Lord. While we were there, someone had played some ungodly secular song on the jukebox several times.

As we were walking out to our cars, we both started singing the chorus of that song! We hadn't even really listened to the song, yet it had penetrated our spirits and was now lingering in our consciousnesses. My mouth automatically started speaking what had been sown in my heart through the gateway of my ears.

That's why you need to be so selective about what type of conversation you permit yourself to hear. You can't hang around with people who talk doubt and unbelief without being adversely affected.

"Oh, Pastor Dollar, I just let that stuff go in one ear and out the other." That's impossible. Just as I ended up singing a song I wasn't even listening to, you'll end up singing your friend's song of doubt and unbelief when times get tough. That which enters your ear penetrates your heart and will eventually end up coming out of your mouth.

You simply must guard your ears. The kind of talk you hear will be what you ultimately believe. Association brings assimilation.

## Faith Cometh

One of the most frequently cited verses of scripture concerning faith is Romans 10:17. Let's look at it in context:

> **How then shall they call on him in whom they have not believed? and how shall they believe in him of whom they have not heard? and how shall**

**they hear without a preacher? And how shall they preach, except they be sent? as it is written, How beautiful are the feet of them that preach the gospel of peace, and bring glad tidings of good things! But they have not all obeyed the gospel. For Esaias saith, Lord, who hath believed our report? So then faith cometh by hearing, and hearing by the word of God. (Romans 10:14-17)**

"Faith cometh by hearing, and hearing by the word of God." We've heard it and said it so often, it's almost become a cliché in many Christian circles. But what does this familiar phrase really mean? Let's look at the Amplified Bible for more light on these verses:

**14 But how are people to call upon Him Whom they have not believed—in Whom they have no faith, on Whom they have no reliance? And how are they to believe in Him—adhere to, trust in and rely upon Him—of Whom they have never heard? And how are they to hear without a preacher?**

**15 And how can men [be expected to] preach unless they are sent? As it is written, How beautiful are the feet of those who bring glad tidings!—How welcome is the coming of those who preach the good news of his good things!**

**16 But they have not all heeded the Gospel; for Isaiah says, Lord who has believed (had faith in) what he has heard from us?**

**17 <u>So faith comes by hearing [what is told], and what is heard comes by the preaching [of the message that came from the lips] of Christ, the Messiah [Himself].</u>**

When verse 14 asks, "...how are they to believe in Him...of whom they have never heard," it introduces a very important spiritual truth. You can't believe in or ask for something that you've never heard preached.

Have you ever noticed that in churches where salvation is never preached, nobody gets saved? In churches where they preach salvation but never healing, people get saved but no one gets healed. Is it any wonder there are so many people who can't pay their bills in churches where they're never told it is God's will for them to prosper?

If you've never heard that God is your deliverer, how can you ever be delivered? You can't believe in something you've never heard proclaimed. That's why it is so important that preachers preach the whole word, from A to Z. As this passage of scripture asks, "How can the people hear without a preacher?"

Then it asks another question. "How can men preach unless they are sent?"

Some preachers are sent, commissioned and ordained by God. Others just go in their own power and strength. When it comes to deciding which preacher you're going to listen to, you've got to know the difference between the "sent" one and the "went" one.

When God sends you to do something, He provides all the necessary equipment and ability to get the job done. If I send my son to the store for groceries, I'm going to give him enough money to buy the things for which I've sent him. The same principle holds true for preachers.

The "went" one who takes off on his own initiative because he thinks it's a good idea probably won't have the equipment he needs. Preachers, you must be equipped. And you will be, if you are truly sent.

Why is it one man can get up and preach a sermon with tremendous, life-changing results in the lives of the hearers, while another can get up and preach the same sermon with no results? It's the difference between the sent one and the went one.

That's why you have to be discerning even when it comes to Christian radio and television. Some believers think they're doing a good thing by tuning in to a Christian station and just leaving it on. In reality, a lot of doubt, unbelief and bad teaching may be bombarding your ears if you do that.

You must guard your heart with all diligence, for out of it come the forces of life (Proverbs 4:23).

### You Need a Fresh Hearing

Let's look at old familiar Romans 10:17 one more time.

*So then faith cometh by hearing, and hearing by the word of God.*

Please understand what the Word is saying here. If you are sick and need faith to get healed, faith comes by hearing the Word of God concerning healing. It does you no good to hear the Word concerning finances if you have cancer. Nor does it help to hear the Word on healing when you need money.

Faith for whatever you need comes from hearing and acting on the Word that specifically deals with that particular need.

It's also important to understand that faith doesn't come from having heard. It comes from "hearing"—present tense. Some people think because they heard "By His stripes you were healed" many years ago, they have the faith to be healed today. It simply doesn't work that way.

Just because you put gas in your car last month or even last week, doesn't mean you have the fuel to get you where you need to go. Gas to get you to work this week comes by stopping and pumping a fresh tank-full.

The memory of yesterday's meal won't strengthen and nourish you for today's activity. You are going to have to have another meal. It may be the same stuff you ate yesterday, but you still must eat again.

The same is true of hearing the Word. You need a fresh hearing to receive faith for today's needs. I don't care how many times you've heard a certain verse—you may be able to quote it backwards, forwards and in your sleep—if it speaks to a present problem, you need to see it in your own Bible, say it with your own mouth and hear it preached by a man of God.

When sickness tries to attack my body, the first thing I do is get my healing tapes out and start listening to them. I open my Bible, look up all the verses on healing and read them aloud.

Faith is not a one time event. It is a life. It is a process that we do over and over again. You'll never win a battle on the shells you fired in the last war. When a new enemy comes, it's time to reload. Reloading the gun of faith comes by hearing and hearing by the Word of God.

### Be a Good Receiver

Not only is it vital that you hear the Word when you're facing a problem, it is important to hear it properly. *How* you receive God's Word can make an enormous difference in the results you see.

That is precisely what Jesus was saying in Mark 4:24 right after he gave the parable of the sower and the soils:

> **And he said unto them, Take heed what ye hear: with what measure ye mete, it shall be measured to you: and unto you that hear shall more be given.**

Once again we're warned: "take heed what you hear." Don't allow just anything to go through the gate of your ears. If you're trying to get healed, whatever you do, don't let your relatives sit around your bed telling you how bad you look. If you are trying to build a prosperous business, don't sit around listening to people talk about how terrible the economy is.

Why? Because fear cometh by hearing, and hearing by the word of the enemy. Fear is the reciprocal of faith. And as powerful as faith is to do you good, fear is powerful to open you up to harm.

Take another look at the last half of that verse.

**...with what measure ye mete, it shall be measured to you: and unto you that hear shall more be given.**

This applies the law of sowing and reaping to the act of hearing the Word of God. The more attention and weight you give to the Word, the more revelation and power you're going to receive. Those who learn to hear will hear more and more.

In other words, not only will you get results from your hearing of the Word, you'll get revelation, too! And Jesus said the very gates of hell cannot prevail against the rock of personal revelation (Matthew 16:18).

## Fall In Love with the Word

There is no way to over-emphasize the importance of hearing, and hearing, and hearing the Word of God. In John 8:47, Jesus tells us, "He that is of God heareth God's words; ye therefore hear them not, because ye are not of God." He's saying, "If you're of God, hear my Word."

Few things in your Christian walk will benefit you more than simply falling in love with God's Word. Hear the Word as you read it. Hear it on television, tapes, and radio. Hear it preached by an anointed man or woman of God in church. Just hear it.

This is never more vital than when you are facing a problem or need. Go to the Word and find a promise that directly answers that problem. Then hear it, hear it, and hear it some more. It's a powerful and absolutely essential step in God's plan for getting you from the problem to the answer.

# Chapter 7
# Step Five: Success Through Meditation

**This book of the law shall not depart out of thy mouth; but thou shalt meditate therein day and night... (Joshua 1:6)**

Thus far in our examination of God's divine order of faith, we've established several important biblical truths. One is that God's Word is spiritual "seed" which has the potential to germinate into whatever you need in your life. Another is that "hearing" is necessary to access that seed.

Now we'll see in the Word that the key to planting that seed in your heart, where it can do some good, is *meditation*.

Let me say at the outset that "meditation" is a subject which is often misunderstood and unnecessarily controversial. When some people hear the word meditation, they instantly assume you're talking about some Eastern mystical occult practice brought to America by Buddhists. Let me assure you, I'm not.

That kind of meditation is a counterfeit—a perversion of something God created for His people to use. You see, Satan can't create anything. He can only twist things God has created.

As we'll see in this chapter, meditation is a Bible word. We're not taking a tool from the devil's kingdom and trying to use it for God. We're simply rediscovering a powerful God-given method for getting His Word deep into our hearts and spirits.

Certainly there are a lot of people in the occult using Satan's perverted form of meditation. And they're getting perverted, destructive results as they do.

In this chapter you'll discover God's purpose for meditation, how your imagination plays a role in getting from the problem to the answer, and how to put these tools to use to bring phenomenal results in your prayer life.

## Imagine That

At the most basic level, to meditate means to dwell on something in thought. It involves turning or revolving a concept or thought in your mind in order to see it from different angles. It means to ponder. In addition, real Bible meditation involves the use of the imagination. When you imagine something you see it in your "mind's eye."

The imagination, a God-created part of every one of us, is a faculty we haven't heard much Bible teaching about. Yet it's one of the most powerful instruments we possess for getting results. They may be perverted, wicked results, given the way most people use their imaginations, but results just the same.

If, however, we can uncover God's created purpose for the imagination and begin to use it the way He intended, we'll begin to get astounding, righteous results.

I probably don't have to tell you your imagination can get you into trouble. Unholy imaginations and fantasies have led many a person into dangerous waters. But did you know using your imagination God's way can get you healed, delivered, and blessed? It can! But only when used in the context of God's divine order of faith.

## I Can See It!

How many times have you walked by a department store window, looked at a dress or a suit and remarked, "Man, I can see myself wearing that!" Have you ever been passed by a new car and muttered, "Hey, I can see myself driving something like that."

The fact is, you really did see yourself driving that car. How? In your mind's eye. Through the faculty of your imagination you were able to see a reality that didn't currently exist. This ability has many spiritual applications.

"But Pastor Dollar, the Bible doesn't say anything about imagination, does it?" Oh, but it does! In fact, it says plenty. One of the first scriptural references to the imagination occurs in Genesis. Let's look:

> **And they said, Go to, let us build us a city and a tower, whose top may reach unto heaven; and let us make us a name, lest we be scattered abroad upon the face of the whole earth. And the LORD came down to see the city and the tower, which the children of men builded. And the LORD said, Behold, the people is one, and they have all one language; and this they begin to do: and now nothing will be restrained from them, which they have imagined to do. (Genesis 11:4-6)**

Here we have a group of ungodly, rebellious people. But because they were unified in purpose and language God said they could accomplish anything they could *imagine*. Nothing could hold them back.

Why was their potential so great? Because of their unity and because of a blueprint in their imaginations. You see, you can't build a building without a blueprint.

The nearly unlimited power of unity and imagination got God's immediate attention. God, in effect, said, "I've got to put a stop to this. With the blueprint they have imagined, it won't be long until I've got a tower sticking up through my living room!"

Of course, I'm being facetious. But the fact remains, God came down and confound their language in order to destroy their unity, because imagination is such a powerful tool. If you can learn to use it God's way, it will become a formidable weapon in your spiritual arsenal.

Sadly, up to this point most believers have been wasting this awesome creative tool by meditating on junk, or even worse, things that are unclean and sinful. Yet, as we're about to see, God's plan is for you to use meditation as a means of overcoming.

### Good Success

Now that we have at least a surface understanding of what meditation is, let's find out what the Bible has to say about how to use it:

> **This book of the law [God's Word] shall not depart out of thy mouth; but thou shalt meditate therein day and night, that thou mayest observe to do according to all that is written therein: for then thou shalt make thy way prosperous, and then thou shalt have good success. (Joshua 1:8)**

Let's break this verse down and get some understanding of God's purpose for meditation.

First, it says, "This book of the law shall not depart out of thy mouth..." God's law is His Word. His Word is His law. Therefore the book of the law, for us, refers to God's Word, the Bible. Here, we're told to speak it all the time. That confirms what we discovered in the previous chapter about the importance of hearing yourself speak the Word.

The next part says, "...but thou shalt meditate therein day and night..." In other words, take God's Word and ponder it. Dwell on it. Take it and turn it over and around in your mind. Use your imagination to "see" yourself doing that Word.

What does meditating the Word day and night empower you to do? You meditate so "...thou mayest observe to do according to all that is written therein." Basically, it enables you to live what you see in your Bible.

Have you ever been challenged by something you saw in the Word? Have you ever read a biblical command and thought, "I can't do that!"? I'd venture to say you have. I've not yet met a believer who got saved and immediately started walking in obedience to everything he or she saw in scripture.

Most of us, when stepping out to a new level of commitment or faith, face fear. Fear that God's Word won't work for us like it does others. Fear that God won't come through. We just can't "see" ourselves doing that part of the Word.

For instance, when some Christians read Malachi 3:10 and discover they're supposed to tithe, they are gripped with fear. "I can't afford to tithe!" they tell themselves. The devil, always willing to lend a helping hand, whispers, "That's right. You can't pay your bills as it is. How are you going to make it if you give ten percent to God?"

The problem here is that the believer can't "see" himself tithing and prospering as a result. That's where meditation of the Word comes in. Remember, Joshua 1:8 said meditate day and night "that thou mayest observe to do according to all that is written therein.."

That's the key! For example, as you meditate Malachi 3:10...

**Bring ye all the tithes into the storehouse, that there may be meat in mine house, and prove me now herewith, saith the LORD of hosts, if I will not open you the windows of heaven, and pour you out a blessing, that there shall not be room enough to receive it.**

...you begin to see the windows of heaven opening up and pouring out blessings. The more you meditate the truth of this scripture, the more real and vivid the image becomes. Eventually you can clearly see yourself tithing and being blessed. Ultimately fear is completely displaced by faith. You're a tither!

This principle works for anything you can see in the Word. And the result is always the same:

**...for then thou shalt make thy way prosperous, and then thou shalt have good success.**

Prosperity and success are the inevitable by-products of being a meditator-doer of God's Word.

### Plant It

The Bible is loaded with promises of blessing and increase for those who will invest time in meditating the Word. You'll find one such promise in Psalm 1:1-3:

> **Blessed is the man that walketh not in the counsel of the ungodly, nor standeth in the way of sinners, nor sitteth in the seat of the scornful. But his delight is in the law of the LORD; and in his law doth he meditate day and night. And he shall be like a tree planted by the rivers of water, that bringeth forth his fruit in his season; his leaf also shall not wither; and whatsoever he doeth shall prosper.**

Who is this well-watered, fruit-bearing person who prospers in everything he or she does? The one who delights and meditates God's Word day and night!

The Word is seed. If you want a harvest of blessing and victory you must take it out of the bag (the Bible) and plant it in the soil of your heart through meditation.

This is where so many believers miss it. They confuse reading or memorizing scripture with meditating it. Reading and memorization are wonderful but they don't plant the seed of the Word in your heart like meditation does. The first two put the Word in your head; the other, in your heart.

Only when you've planted can you rightfully expect the fruit of the harvest. No farmer in his right mind stands over his fields waiting for a harvest when the seed is still in sacks in the barn. But once he has sown the seed in good soil, he has every reason to expect fruit.

Many Christians are waiting for the Word to produce in their lives when they've never truly sown it in their hearts. Sure, they've heard it preached. They've read it many times. They may even have lots of verses memorized. But until it's planted in the fertile soil of an obedient heart, their expectation is in vain.

## How to Meditate the Word

Okay. Let's get practical. I am going to give you three down-to-earth methods of meditating God's Word you can start using today. The good news is, none of them require you to sit in the lotus position and hum.

### 1. Mutter

Have you ever found yourself walking around muttering something under your breath in a time of stress or irritation? You may not have realized it, but you were practicing a negative form of meditation. One of the meanings of the Hebrew word translated "meditate" in the Bible literally means "to speak to oneself."

A highly effective method of meditation involves simply speaking a verse (or even a two or three-word phrase from a verse) to yourself.

"But won't my family and friends think I've lost my marbles if I go around mumbling to myself?" you ask.

They won't after they start seeing the phenomenal change in your life it brings about. Besides, speaking to yourself is perfectly biblical. Paul even suggests it!

> **Speaking to yourselves in psalms and hymns and spiritual songs, singing and making melody in your heart to the Lord... (Ephesians 5:19)**

There you have it. It's even in the New Testament. Speaking or singing the Word to yourself is an excellent way to meditate the things of God.

### 2. Talk it.

A second way to meditate the Word is to just plain speak it out. That's the basic meaning of the word "meditate" we read in Joshua 1:8.

Talking the Word and its principles out loud, either to God or to another person, has a powerful effect on your heart and spirit. As you can see in the following verses, words and meditation are closely linked:

**I will meditate also of all thy work, and talk of thy doings. (Psalm 77:12)**

**Let the words of my mouth, and the meditation of my heart, be acceptable in thy sight, O LORD, my strength, and my redeemer. (Psalm 19:14)**

**My mouth shall speak of wisdom; and the meditation of my heart shall be of understanding. (Psalm 49:3)**

If you and I go to lunch and talk about God's faithfulness to meet all our needs, that conversation stirs up the Word within me and plants more of it in my heart. That works in the negative, too.

If you go around talking about how big a failure you are, then it won't be long until you start expecting failure, because seeds of failure have been sown in your heart. Failure has been your meditation.

This is why God is so opposed to sins of the tongue: gossip, backbiting, slander, and the like. Those words are a form of meditation that sink into your heart like poison. "The words of a talebearer are as wounds, and they go down into the innermost parts of the belly [heart] (Proverbs 18:8).

### 3. Musing

The third method of effective meditation is the one more commonly associated with the Word. It is musing over or pondering something from the Word. It's the type of meditation described in Psalm 143:5:

**I remember the days of old; I meditate on all thy works; I muse on the work of thy hands.**

I liken this kind of meditation to squeezing juice out of an orange. You may take a single phrase such as, "By His stripes I am healed," and ponder it over and over and over again until it becomes absolutely real on the inside of you. You squeeze until there's not another drop left.

Make no mistake about it, this requires considerable effort and self-discipline. There is no lazy way into the deep things of God. Far too many Christians today have developed a welfare mentality where spiritual things are concerned. They want everything served up on a platter, and cooked in the microwave!)

Yes it's hard, but oh, the rewards are great. I challenge anyone to try the things I've talked about here for seven days. There's no question whatsoever in my mind that it will revolutionize your spiritual life. You'll experience more power, more answered prayer, more revelation... more everything.

Still, only a handful of Christians ever muster the energy to pay the price for such abundant life. Instead, they go begging God for success or healing or whatever it is they need. All the while, the key to the storehouse of heaven is in their hands.

"Pastor Dollar, I'm still not sure I really understand how to meditate." Then permit me to bring it right down to where you live.

Go to the Scripture and find a verse or passage that addresses a current need. Spend 15 or 20 minutes meditating it. Say it quietly to yourself. Ponder it. Consider it. Close your eyes and see yourself doing or experiencing that scripture.

Throughout the day turn to your spouse or friend and make a declaration based on that scripture (e.g., God is supplying all my needs according to His riches in glory"). Continue to ponder the verse or phrase as you lay down at night. Your spirit will continue to soak in revelation even while you sleep.

When you wake up, take the same scripture and start the process again. Mutter it to yourself. Say it to others. Muse on it at every opportunity. As you do, that truth will become more and more alive in your spirit, and that seed will be planted more deeply in your heart.

If you will really give this approach a try, you'll find it's the most powerful thing you've ever done. Sure, it takes self-discipline. Yes, it requires concentration and commitment. But the rewards are abundant life, victory, health, prosperity, success, and the most precious reward of all—greater intimacy with your Heavenly Father.

Meditation is the indispensable fifth step in God's divine order of faith.

# Chapter 8
# Step Six: Harness the Power of Confession

**For with the heart man believeth unto righteousness; and with the mouth confession is made unto salvation. (Romans 10:10)**

The sixth step in God's infallible formula for getting you from the problem to the solution is—confession.

You may be thinking, "Oh, I know all about that confession stuff. It doesn't work for me." If you think so, you're not alone. People who have heard and received good faith teaching get hung up and frustrated in this area more than any other. The reason is simple.

As I've been saying throughout this entire book, there is an established, God-ordained order to the things of faith. You simply cannot scramble God's divine order of faith in any way you please and expect to get results. Nor can you pick and choose among these ten steps as if you were in a cafeteria line.

This is doubly true when it comes to confession. So many believers have grabbed on to one little piece of something they heard Kenneth Hagin or Kenneth Copeland say regarding confessing what they desire without hearing the whole teaching. Then they run out and start saying, "I have a new car," 400 times a day and get irritated when nothing seems to happen after a week.

Is confession a powerful tool? Yes! Can it bring you tremendous, supernatural results? Absolutely! But only when preceded and followed by the proper steps in God's order. Let's discover how to harness the awesome power of confession.

## First Things First

Before we move on to learning how confession is used, let's find out what it is. Defined simply, confession is "using the mouth to bring forth." It is more than just "saying" something. It means "to declare a thing in order to establish or confirm it." True confession is an authoritative spiritual proclamation.

A good way to think about effective confession is in terms of firing a gun. A gun that fires blanks sounds the same as one that fires real bullets. They both go "boom!" Yet one is effective; the other just makes noise.

If you've got a snake in your yard, you can fire blanks at it all day long and never kill the thing. However, one real bullet will take care of that slimy serpent in no time.

That's why so many Christians have gotten frustrated with confession. The devil (a serpent) is loose in their finances, health or family. They are firing the gun of confession—they are saying the right words—yet nothing is happening. Why? They're firing blanks. The gun of confession hasn't been loaded with the right ammunition.

This explains why one person can say, "That car is mine, in the name of Jesus," and get it; while another says the exact same thing but is still taking the bus to work.

## Effective Confession

Make no mistake about it—words are powerful things. Hebrews 11:3 tells us, "the worlds were framed [built] by the word of God." Read the first two chapters of Genesis and you'll see that's true.

For example, Genesis 1:3 says:

**And God said, Let there be light: and there was light.**

You'll see that phrase, "And God said," repeated again in verses 6, 9, 11, 14, 20, 24, 26, and 29. Each time God wanted to create something new, he *said* something. Don't try to tell me words aren't important. I know better.

Look again at verse 3. A literal Hebrew translation of that verse would more accurately read:

**Light in me, be: and light was.**

Where did the light that was created come from? From inside God! He spoke (or confessed) what was already a reality in His heart.

If confession is the gun, words based on an already present inner reality are the bullets. What then, is the gunpowder that fills and propels those bullets? Why, the substance of faith, of course!

This is how all these forces and vehicles interact to produce results and why it is so important to have things in the proper order before you go "shooting your mouth off." Far too often we've hurried to fire the gun of confession without doing what is necessary to load it with a clear inner image (the bullet) and to fill that image with faith (the gunpowder).

Other times we've had a loaded gun (a clear inner image and faith) but have neglected to pull the trigger through the exercise of confession!

Getting all of these elements together is not as difficult as it may seem. In fact, if you follow the steps we've outlined thus far, you're already set to take aim and fire.

### Building a Clear Inner Image

If you ever want to start seeing what you say, you're going to have to learn to create it in your heart first. How do you do that? By diligently doing what we learned in the previous step—meditating the appropriate parts of God's Word.

Meditating the Word of God builds a clear image in your heart of the thing for which you are believing. This is why God was able to say, "Light in me, be," when He wanted light to be manifested in the physical universe. His confession simply released what had already been created in His heart.

That's where meditation on the Word of God comes in for the believer. Say, for instance, you need healing. If you will begin meditating on what God's Word has to say about healing—mutter, speak, and muse "By His stripes I am healed, eventually an image of a healed "you" will begin to take shape in your heart.

Once you've done that, then and only then do you get the healing out of your heart and into the physical realm of your body through the instrument of confession.

If you've been "confessing" that all your needs are met in Christ Jesus, but your phone's been disconnected, your electricity is cut off, and they're carrying your furniture away, perhaps it's because you've never really taken the time to build a clear image of "all-sufficiency" in your heart.

Your mouth confession and your heart meditation go hand in hand. One won't work independently of the other.

## Timing is Everything

The most common mistake Christians make in the area of confession is failing to wait until "the gun" is fully loaded before squeezing the trigger. God gives us a great illustration of the power of waiting in Joshua chapter 6, in which Israel is preparing to take the walled city of Jericho.

If you are familiar with the account, you'll remember that God instructed Joshua to have Israel march around the city seven times a day for six days. Furthermore, He commanded them to be silent as they did so:

> **And Joshua had commanded the people, saying, Ye shall not shout, nor make any noise with your voice, neither shall any word proceed out of your mouth, until the day I bid you shout; then shall ye shout. (Joshua 6:10)**

Why do you think God had the Israelites march around silently for six days before he would allow them to let go a victory shout? So they would meditate as they marched.

With each passing day they developed a clearer inner image of those walls lying on the ground and that city under their control.

When finally, on the seventh day, on the seventh trip around the walls, Joshua gave the order to shout, their confession was so loaded with faith's substance that it literally blew those massive walls down.

Now, seven is the biblical number of completion or perfection. What God is saying here is, "Don't open your mouth until your meditation of my Word is complete."

Once the reality of God's promise is more real on the inside of you than your outward circumstances, you can't help but shout your victory. That's when the walls of whatever is opposing you will crumble like sand.

I've experienced this personally. I remember once when I had been diagnosed with meningitis. I put my healing tapes on and got my healing scriptures out. At that point I wasn't making any bold confessions. I just kept my mouth shut and meditated.

I muttered and mused those healing scriptures until I was so full of the reality of healing that it was coming out of my hair. Then, when I knew that I knew it was real, I stood right up in the middle of my bed and shouted, "I AM HEALED!!!"

My symptoms didn't disappear that very instant but that didn't matter. I knew I was healed. And, of course, I was. My healing manifested in my physical body very quickly. The key was doing the hard work of meditation before moving on to the step of proclaiming my confession.

### Summing Up the Heart-Mouth Connection

Child of God, the Lord created your heart and your mouth to be married. When you try to use one independently of the other, it's like a type of adultery. That's precisely what many of us have been trying to do in the area of confession.

This linkage of heart and mouth is never seen more clearly than in Romans 10:9,10:

> **That if thou shalt confess with thy mouth the Lord Jesus, and shalt believe in thine heart that God hath raised him from the dead, thou shalt be saved. For with the heart man believeth unto righteousness; and with the mouth confession is made unto salvation. (Romans 10:9-10)**

God created the mouth and the heart to work as a team. They are the "dynamic duo."

Don't try to move into confession with the mouth until you've established belief in the heart. Once you've done both, you're ready to move up to the next rung on the ladder of faith.

# Chapter 9
# Step Seven: Acting on the Word

**And why call ye me Lord, Lord, and do not the things which I say? (Luke 6:46)**

So far, we've talked about the importance of identifying your problem and finding your "title deed" to a solution in the Word. We've also talked about hearing the Word, meditating the Word and finally confessing the Word.

Once you've taken these vital steps, it's time to go on to the next one—acting on the Word. This is another place where many Christians tend to short-circuit the power of faith before they ever see any results. And nobody in the Bible makes a stronger case for acting on your faith than James. Read this familiar passage:

**What doth it profit, my brethren, though a man say he hath faith, and have not works? can faith save him? If a brother or sister be naked, and destitute of daily food, And one of you say unto them, Depart in peace, be ye warmed and filled; notwithstanding ye give them not those things which are needful to the body; what doth it profit? Even so faith, if it hath not works, is dead, being alone. Yea, a man may say, Thou hast faith, and I have works: shew me thy faith without thy works, and I will shew thee my faith by my works. Thou believest that there is one God; thou doest well: the devils also believe, and tremble. But wilt thou know, O vain man, that faith without works is dead? Was not Abraham our father justified by works, when he had offered Isaac his son upon the altar? Seest thou how faith wrought with his works, and by works was faith made perfect? And the scripture was fulfilled which saith, Abraham believed God, and it**

**was imputed unto him for righteousness: and he was called the Friend of God. Ye see then how that by works a man is justified, and not by faith only. Likewise also was not Rahab the harlot justified by works, when she had received the messengers, and had sent them out another way? For as the body without the spirit is dead, so faith without works is dead also. (James 2:14-26)**

Here, in no uncertain terms, James tells us, "Faith without works is dead." It's one of the most frequently quoted phrases in all of the Scripture. It also happens to be very true. You can generate faith by hearing the Word of God, plant that faith in your heart by meditating on it, even put it into motion by confessing it. But unless you take the additional step of acting on it, there's no life in it to produce the thing you need.

A literal Greek translation of the word "works" in that verse is "corresponding action." Therefore it is accurate to say that faith without corresponding action is dead.

If you really believe all your needs are met according to God's riches in glory by Christ Jesus, you'll act like it. Likewise, true faith in Jesus as your healer will produce a corresponding action. Living, moving, producing faith will always be accompanied by corresponding action. It's a principle we see repeated in scripture over and over.

### Faith in Action

James gives us several outstanding examples of people who backed up their faith with deeds. One of them is Abraham.

You'll remember that he and Sarah were given a miracle baby by God when Abraham was 100 years old. Later God spoke to him and asked him to take his son, Isaac, and sacrifice him on an altar.

Now, Abraham knew God had promised that through Isaac, he would be the father of many nations (Genesis 17:4). He had meditated on the stars of the sky and the sand of the sea while developing an inner image of all the descendants he would have one day (Genesis 22:17). He had spoken and confessed that his very name was Father of a Multitude (Genesis 17:5). He had taken every step we've seen so far in God's divine order of faith. So when the time came to put his faith into action, notice what he says:

> **And Abraham said unto his young men, Abide ye here with the ass; and I and the lad will go yonder and worship, and come again to you. (Genesis 22:5)**

Did you see that? "I and the lad will go...and come again to you." Abraham did more than talk his faith in God's promise, he was willing to stake his all on it. And he did.

Abraham was more than just a hearer of the Word. He was a doer. His reward was a miraculous realization of the promises of God. Keep in mind, however, Abraham had done all the other steps of faith up to this point. That's the difference between Abraham's experience and a lot of the so called faith failures you hear so much about.

Many people who are sick hear a little bit about faith, read "By His stripes I am healed," and confess it a couple of times. Then they hear they're supposed to act on their faith, so they throw their medicine away. When they almost die, they wonder why that faith stuff didn't work for them.

God is being blamed for a lot of faith failures by people who simply didn't know or bother to operate under God's divine order concerning faith. Is it important to act on the Word? Yes! It's essential. But only after you've laid the foundation by doing the previous six steps we've discussed.

Don't blame God if you ignore his established order and things don't work out. For example, nowhere in God's Word does it tell anyone to stop taking their medicine. And no, it's not a sin to go to the doctor. Don't let anyone tell you it is. God is still the healer whether healing is facilitated by a medical doctor or worked directly by the Great Physician.

The important point to remember is, once you've laid the groundwork for appropriating a promise from God's Word, it is vital that you carry it on through by acting as if that promise were already a full-blown reality in your life.

Let me give you a practical example. Say for instance, you see in the Word that you are to prosper and have an abundance. You see that you are to be the head and not the tail. The lender and not the borrower. Don't wait until your bank accounts start filling up to begin acting like a prosperous person. Act like one now.

You may not have a lot of fancy new clothes but you can keep the ones you have clean and looking their best. Simply begin thinking like a prosperous person, talking like a prosperous person, and acting like a prosperous person.

In other words, don't wait until you see the abundance to start walking in abundance. People with plenty of money don't worry about money all the time. They don't go around crying to everyone about how they can't pay their bills. And if you're expecting God's Word to be a reality in your life, neither should you!

Does that mean you should go out and charge up all your credit cards and go into debt in order to look more successful than your really are? Of course not. I'm talking about a change in attitude—an adjustment in lifestyle and outlook. I'm talking about grabbing hold of a promise in God's Word and acting like it is so.

Don't think for a minute that such a shift in behavior will come easily. Old habits and thinking patterns die hard. Furthermore, when some of your friends and family see you walking in a reality they can't yet see, they may give you a hard time. Ignore them. They won't be laughing when the manifestation of God's promise is apparent for all the world to see.

## Believing You Receive

This business of acting as if the promise were already manifested is intricately tied to an important principle found in Mark 11:23,24. Let's look at these amazing words of Jesus:

> **For verily I say unto you, That whosoever shall say unto this mountain, Be thou removed, and be thou cast into the sea; and shall not doubt in his heart, but shall believe that those things which he saith shall come to pass; he shall have whatsoever he saith. Therefore I say unto you, What things soever ye desire, when ye pray, believe that ye receive them, and ye shall have them.**

Look at that last line as it is translated in the NIV. "Therefore I tell you, whatever you ask for in prayer, believe that you have received it, and it will be yours."

"Believe that you have received it." In a sense, that's another way of saying, "It's yours in the spiritual realm, so start acting like it, and you'll see it in the physical realm!"

That means when you've got a bill due that you can't pay, you read, hear, and meditate Philippians 4:19 ("My God shall supply all my needs...") until it's an inner reality. Then you go to God in prayer and say "I believe I receive this bill paid now in the name of Jesus Christ."

Now, if you really did believe you received when you prayed, as Mark 11:24 commands, how will you act when you get up off your knees? Why, you'll act as if that bill is paid! You'll think like it's paid. You'll talk like it's paid. You'll rest like it's paid.

Your flesh wants to see the bill paid before it acts like it's paid. The kingdom of God doesn't work that way. We walk by faith, not by sight (II Corinthians 5:7).

A change of action must always precede a change of situation, not the other way around. When you're acting on real faith, your outward circumstances will begin to be shaped by your belief and actions.

Start developing a belief that you are walking in the blessings of God. Cultivate a strong Word-based conviction that God's favor is upon you and goes before you. Then start acting as if those things are so. It will absolutely turn your life around.

### Half-hearted Obedience

Not only does the Bible give us some great examples of people who acted on the Word, it also shows us some who didn't and missed a blessing as a result.

For instance, one of the first times the disciples ever met Jesus they had an opportunity to act on a word from Him. Look at how they responded:

> **Now when he [Jesus] had left speaking, he said unto Simon, Launch out into the deep, and let down your nets for a draught [catch]. And Simon answering said unto him, Master, we have toiled all the night, and have taken nothing: nevertheless at thy word I will let down the net. (Luke 5:4-5)**

Notice the exact wording of Jesus' command—"let down your nets [plural] for a catch." Yet Peter's response was, "I will let down the net [singular]."

Now Peter is thinking, "What does this carpenter know about fishing? I'm the expert on fishing here and I didn't catch anything all night long. But I'll throw out one net just to humor the preacher." You know the result:

> **And when they had this done, they inclosed a great multitude of fishes: and their net brake. And they beckoned unto their partners, which were in the other ship, that they should come and help them. And they came, and filled both the ships, so that they began to sink. (Luke 5:6-7)**

Half-hearted obedience is no obedience at all. Jesus' desire was to bless these men—to provide them with such an enormous catch that they could afford to take an entire year off work and follow him. That's precisely what would have happened had they acted on His Word and taken every net they owned.

Partial action in faith will yield some results. Total action will yield great results.

Another classic biblical example of reluctance to act on the Word is Naaman in the book of II Kings. You'll recall Naaman was a Gentile army general from Syria who was stricken with leprosy, a hideous and incurable disease:

> **Now Naaman, captain of the host of the king of Syria, was a great man with his master, and honourable, because by him the LORD had given deliverance unto Syria: he was also a mighty man in valour, but he was a leper. (II Kings 5:1)**

Eventually, Naaman hears about a great man of God, Elisha, who might be able to miraculously cure his disease, so he pays Elisha a visit:

> **So Naaman came with his horses and with his chariot, and stood at the door of the house of Elisha. (v. 9)**

He found Elisha willing to help him, but when he heard the prophet's prescription, he got offended:

> **And Elisha sent a messenger unto him, saying, Go and wash in Jordan seven times, and thy flesh shall come again to thee, and thou shalt be clean. But Naaman was wroth, and went away, and said, Behold, I thought, He will surely come out to me, and stand, and call on the name of the LORD his God, and strike his hand over the place, and recover the leper. Are not Abana and Pharpar, rivers of Damascus, better than all the waters of Israel? may I not wash in them, and be clean? So he turned and went away in a rage. (v. 10-12)**

Elisha's response outraged Naaman for several reasons. First, Naaman was an important foreign dignitary, and here this country preacher doesn't even bother to come out and meet him!

Secondly, he expected a miracle-worker to come out and do a dance around him or perform some spectacular ceremony. Instead, he was told to go dip himself in the muddy, nasty old Jordan. He walked away angry and just as sick as when he came.

If it hadn't been for some wise encouragement and reasoning from one of his servants, Naaman would have died of that awful plague. Ultimately, he swallowed his pride, acted on the word from God's man and received his miracle:

> **And his servants came near, and spake unto him, and said, My father, if the prophet had bid thee do some great thing, wouldest thou not have done it? how much rather then, when he saith to thee, Wash, and be clean? Then went he down, and dipped himself seven times in Jordan, according to the saying of the man of God: and his flesh came again like unto the flesh of a little child, and he was clean. (v. 13-14)**

I see lots of Christians who act just like Naaman. They have a great need but refuse to walk in simple obedience to God's Word. They want the pastor to personally pray over them, and then they get offended when he tells them to speak to an anointed staff member or counselor instead.

They have a pre-set image in their mind of how they want their deliverance to come. If God's Word calls for anything other than their predetermined plan, they walk away, angry at God, the pastor, and the church.

Simple, child-like obedience to the Word of God will never be unproductive or go unrewarded. Simply hear the Word of the Lord and act on it, no matter how foolish or insignificant it may seem.

## The Right Foundation

In Luke 6, Jesus bluntly told a group of listeners, "Don't call me Lord if you're not going to do what I say:

> **And why call ye me, Lord, Lord, and do not the things which I say. Whosoever cometh to me, and heareth my sayings, and doeth them, I will shew you to whom he is like: He is like a man which built an house, and digged deep, and laid the foundation on a rock: and when the flood arose, the stream beat vehemently upon that house, and could not shake it: for it was founded upon a rock. But he that heareth, and doeth not, is like a man that without a foundation built an house upon the earth; against which the stream did beat vehemently, and immediately it fell; and the ruin of that house was great. (Luke 6:46-49)**

If you will purpose to become a person who not only hears God's Word but does it as well, no storm in life can ever shake you. Nothing the devil can throw at you can ever get the upper hand. Your life will be founded on the immovable rock of obedience to Jesus Christ.

Acting on the Word. It's another crucial step in getting from any problem to God's wonderful answer.

# Chapter 10
# Step Eight: Applying the Pressure of Patience

**That ye be not slothful, but followers of them who through faith and patience inherit the promises. (Hebrews 6:12)**

Although this book is dedicated to laying out the ten steps of faith that will produce an answer to any problem, you should be aware that you may not always get through all ten steps before your answer appears.

Sometimes your faith will produce after doing only the first four or five steps. Other problems may surrender after you've taken the seven steps we've discussed up to this point.

From time to time however, you'll encounter a situation that requires more. That's when you need to be prepared to take the next step in God's divine order of faith—applying the pressure of patience.

## Patience: More Than "Putting Up with It"

When most of us hear the word patience, we think in terms of "putting up with" or "enduring" something. If you're caught in traffic, you remind yourself to "have patience" and that you'll get there eventually. If your boss assigns you to work with an extremely irritating person for a month, you force a smile and say, "I can deal with it. I'm a patient person."

But when the Bible talks about patience, it is referring to something entirely different. Bible patience isn't gritting your teeth and bearing some unpleasant or painful burden. In fact, trouble, irritation, pain, and affliction are always from the devil and should be strenuously resisted by every believer. When Satan tries to put sickness on you, you're not to put up with it. It's not from God, so kick it out of your life!

Know when God's Word mentions patience, it's talking about the ability to remain constant. A person with Bible patience remains fixed and immovable regardless of how the surrounding circumstances look or feel. Patience stands on the Word of God...no matter what.

This is the very quality James is talking about in the following familiar passage of scripture:

**My brethren, count it all joy when ye fall into divers temptations; Knowing this, that the trying of your faith worketh patience. But let patience have her perfect work, that ye may be perfect and entire, wanting nothing. (James 1:2-4)**

A lot of Christians have misunderstood what these verses are saying. When James says, "...the trying of your faith worketh patience," he's not suggesting that patience is produced or created as a result of the trial, as many people believe. Rather, he is saying, "trouble puts patience to work!"

Why is that a cause for joy? Because patience is a force that can cause you to overcome that trouble. If you're in the midst of a trial, you don't want to put bitterness to work. It has no power to help you. You don't want to employ grief, despair, anger, or guilt, either.

No. Rejoice man or woman of faith when you face a trial, because it puts the power of patience to work on your behalf! That truth is echoed in Romans 5:3-4:

**...but we glory in tribulations also: knowing that tribulation worketh [employs] patience; And patience, experience; and experience, hope...**

That's why James said rejoice when patience is about to come on the scene. Because patience hires experience and experience hires hope. Hope is a powerful thing. It ranks right up there with faith and love (I Corinthians 13:13).

In fact, it was David's experience and hope that gave him such confidence to face the giant, Goliath. He said, "Thy servant slew both the lion and the bear: and this uncircumcised Philistine shall be as one of them, seeing he hath defied the armies of the living God" (I Samuel 17:36).

However, as James points out, it all begins with patience—patience employed for the testing of your faith. Notice what James says next:

**But let patience have her perfect work, that ye may be perfect and entire, wanting nothing. (James 1:4)**

Note that said "let patience..." That suggests you have the ability to either permit or prevent patience from performing her perfect work on your behalf. What is her perfect work? "That you may be perfect [complete] and entire wanting [lacking] nothing."

## Double-minded or Single-Purposed

We just saw in James 1:4 that patience, if allowed to do its work, can put you in a place where you have everything you need.

"So how do I *let* patience work, Pastor Dollar? Do I just sit around and wait for it to happen?"

Not a chance. The very next verses give us some insight into what it takes to put patience to work for you:

**If any of you lack wisdom, let him ask of God, that giveth to all men liberally, and upbraideth not; and it shall be given him. But let him ask in faith, nothing wavering. For he that wavereth is like a wave of the sea driven with the wind and tossed. (James 1:5-6)**

Obviously, when it comes to dealing successfully with trials or troubles, the wisdom of God can be a very precious commodity. As the book of Proverbs indicates again and again, wisdom brings with it success, prosperity, long life, and the knowledge of what to do in any situation.

So what does this verse tell you to do in order to get wisdom? Simply "...ask in faith." That shouldn't come as a surprise. Everything in the Christian life always comes back to faith.

In fact, the next verse delivers a pretty blunt warning for the Christian who doesn't have time "for that faith stuff":

> **For let not that man think that he shall receive any thing of the Lord. A double minded man is unstable in all his ways. (James 1:7-8)**

When you're asking God for something, ask in faith. If you don't, you're fooling yourself if you think God is going to deliver it. It is simply not going to happen. "Without faith it is impossible to please God" (Hebrews 11:6).

How do you ask in faith? It's not that hard, really. Here is how I do it:

> **Father, in the name of Jesus, I need wisdom. According to your Word in James chapter one, you said if any man lacks wisdom let him ask, and you will give it liberally and upbraid not. Lord, I ask in faith right now. I believe I receive what I've asked for according to your Word. Philippians 4:19 says, "my God shall supply all your needs according to His riches in Glory by Christ Jesus." You have said I am to be the head and not the tail. Therefore I have wisdom and all my needs are taken care of. I know you've heard me and I know I have the petition that I have asked. In the name of Jesus, that settles it. Amen.**

Then get up off of your knees and go forward, knowing and acting like you've received. That's asking in faith.

If, on the other hand, you ask timidly and full of doubt, James says you're like a wave of the sea being blown every which way. The wavering man says, "I am healed...No, I think I'm sick...No, I'm healed...Wait a minute, I think I'm sick."

Forget it. Don't expect anything from heaven praying like that. "A double-minded man is unstable in all his ways."

Double-mindedness in a sense is the opposite of patience. You'll remember we defined patience as being mentally fixed and immovable. When you are double-minded, you're being moved in whichever direction the winds of adversity happen to be blowing.

When trouble comes, the battleground of patience truly is the mind. And the mind is part of the "soulish" realm (mind, will, and emotions.) Look in Luke 21:19 at what Jesus said to do when encountering tribulation:

**In your patience possess ye your souls.**

The mind is the arena of faith. If patience is going to be allowed to do its work, there is going to have to be a capturing or arresting of the soulish realm.

Have you ever tried to pray and found it impossible because the traffic in your mind was so noisy? At those times, stay with it. Patience will enable you to possess your soul, or, in other words, help you get your mind to shut up. Then, and only then, are you in a position to get single-minded and to pray in faith.

### Faith's Potent Partner

Inheriting the promises in God's Word is the bottom line to everything you're reading in this book. All these steps represent the God-ordained progression for seeing those glorious promises become a reality in your life. And according to Hebrews 6:12, there are two spiritual forces that work in tandem to make that happen:

**That ye be not slothful, but followers of them who through faith and patience inherit the promises.**

"Faith and patience." My friend and father in the faith, Kenneth Copeland, calls them "the power twins." As this scripture indicates, they work together to bring God's great and precious promises to pass in your life.

Faith without patience is one-legged. They have to be joined together to be truly effective. We see this vital connection echoed in Hebrews 10 as well.

> **Cast not away therefore your confidence, which hath great recompence of reward. For ye have need of patience, that, after ye have done the will of God, ye might receive the promise. For yet a little while, and he that shall come will come, and will not tarry. Now the just shall live by faith: but if any man draw back, my soul shall have no pleasure in him. (Hebrews 10:35-38)**

Many times a believer has cast away his confidence right before his miracle was about to be manifested, simply because he lacked patience. What a tragedy.

If you're standing on the Word for your healing, Satan is going to try to get you to throw your confidence away by intensifying the symptoms. Unless you've got faith and patience working together, you're likely to give up and decide it's not working, often right before faith was about to produce a breakthrough for you.

What is God's prescription for not throwing away your confidence on the brink of a miracle? "You have need of patience..." It's faith's partner that keeps the pressure on the devil until he turns loose and runs for the hills. That's why it's an essential stop on the road to your miracle.

# Chapter 11
# Step Nine: Waiting for God's Timing

**Therefore I will look unto the LORD; I will wait for the God of my salvation: my God will hear me. (Micah 7:7)**

Every step in God's divine order of faith we've looked at thus far has been closely linked and related to the previous one. The ninth step is no exception. It literally uses the previous step, "Applying the Pressure of Patience," as a springboard. It is Learning to Wait for God's Timing.

I can almost hear you groaning. "Oh, no. Not another `wait on the Lord' lecture." I don't know what you've been taught in the past but this is good news and I guarantee you're going to like it. It's just one more weapon in your arsenal for getting victory over every problem you may face.

### A Time and a Season

One of the most important truths you can ever grasp in your Christian life is this: with God, there is an appointed time and a due season for everything. That's the theme of this beautiful passage of scripture from one of the wisest men who ever lived:

**To every thing there is a season, and a time to every purpose under the heaven: A time to be born, and a time to die; a time to plant, and a time to pluck up that which is planted; A time to kill, and a time to heal; a time to break down, and a time to build up; A time to weep, and a time to laugh; a time to mourn, and a time to dance; A time to cast away stones, and a time to gather stones together; a time to embrace, and a time to refrain from embracing; A time to get, and a time to lose; a time to keep, and a time to cast away; A time to rend, and a**

**time to sew; a time to keep silence, and a time to speak; A time to love, and a time to hate; a time of war, and a time of peace. (Ecclesiastes 3:1-8)**

God has an established season of time for every purpose in your life. He sees the end from the beginning and has a master time sheet with ordered seasons for all things to take place.

This is a concept you must keep in mind as you begin to pray and believe for certain things in your life. Often, the things for which you're asking will directly and indirectly affect other believers as well. Our lives are linked in a complex interconnected web. Our Heavenly Father sits above it all, working all things together for our good.

We serve a God not bounded by our concepts of time and distance. That's a lesson he brought home to me very clearly when I was a young believer.

You see, as a very small boy, I would ask why God doesn't have a father. I had a father. My father had a father. Everyone in the world had a father as far as I knew. Who then, I wondered, was God's father? I never got a satisfactory answer from anyone I asked.

Years later, when I began to mature in the Word and develop a relationship with God, I asked Him myself. One day, while praying, I just said point blank, "God, who is your daddy?" I'll never forget His response.

"Son, I created the system you are trying to put me in. I created the system of reproduction in which everything produces after its own kind. I stand outside that system because it came out of me. I AM that I AM, the beginning and the end. I have always been here. You can't put me in time, because time came out of me. Don't put me in anything I created."

"Yes sir, Boss," was my quick reply. But I've never forgotten that truth. I frequently see Christians who need to get that understanding. They have God on their personal timetable. If he doesn't come through when they think

He needs to, they assume something must be wrong somewhere. They need to understand God has a time and purpose for everything under heaven.

You may be wondering about some things today. You may be saying, "Lord, when is my business going to take off?" There is a due season. "Where is the anointing and power to minister I've been praying for?" There is a due season. "Where is the husband I desire so greatly?" Child of God, there is a due season. Your time is coming.

The key to avoiding frustration, fear and the temptation to quit when standing in faith on God's Word is understanding there is a time and due season for everything.

### Your Due Season

As a pastor who has counseled hundreds of believers, one of the things I see regularly is frustration at trying to appropriate the promises of God. Invariably, as I talk with them, I am reminded of Galatians 6:7-9:

> **Be not deceived; God is not mocked: for whatsoever a man soweth, that shall he also reap. For he that soweth to his flesh shall of the flesh reap corruption; but he that soweth to the Spirit shall of the Spirit reap life everlasting. <u>And let us not be weary in well doing: for in due season we shall reap, if we faint not</u>.**

This passage is loaded with truth for the believer trying to get from the problem to the answer. First, we're reminded of the universal law of sowing and reaping. Obviously, this refers to more than just literal seeds. We sow many things in the natural course of daily living. Money, words, attitudes, time, deeds—all, good or bad, are seeds for sowing.

Whatever you are right now is the result of your past sowing. That's difficult for a lot of people to accept. It's much more comfortable to blame others or the devil for all their problems. The fact is, the devil really can't do anything to you until you give him an opening.

I found it to be a very liberating thing when I finally faced the fact that my circumstances today are a product of the kind of seed I sowed yesterday.

However, when it comes to dealing with the frustration so many believers feel concerning the things of faith, it's the last verse in that passage that we really need to consider:

**And let us not be weary in well doing; for in due season we shall reap, if we faint not. (Galatians 6:9)**

This is so important and is precisely where many believers miss it. Somewhere along the road to your answer, the persecution, the affliction, or the seeming lack of results causes you to grow weary.

It has happened to the most seasoned of faith warriors. You can be going strong—reading and meditating God's Word, talking like you're supposed to talk, going where you're supposed to go, praying, fasting, and doing anything else you can think of to do—when suddenly you sit down and realize you're tired.

That is the critical moment. The time you are most tempted to move off of your stand of faith and quit is the time you most need to remember to "not be weary in well-doing." Why? Because you'll reap in due season if you'll just hang on.

Don't get tired of doing, speaking, and living God's Word. Don't get tired of standing for your healing. Don't get tired of tithing and giving. Stay on the Word. Your due season of harvest and blessing is coming. God has appointed it!

## No Cave-Ins

"In due season we shall reap, if we faint not." Where the promises of God are concerned, it's not a matter of "if" He's going to come through, it's only a matter of "when." God only knows how many times you've quit just before your due season arrived.

Now, notice what stops you from reaching your due season. Fainting. That word faint means "to give up, cave-in, or quit."

If you won't cave in under the pressure of circumstances and mocking voices, you will reap. Don't stop. Your answer is on its way.

"But I'm not seeing any progress!" What we often don't realize is that progress is being made in the spiritual realm that we simply can't see until it suddenly breaks forth. A lot can be happening beneath the surface that you never perceive if you just go by what you can see.

Don't quit because your mountain doesn't seem to be moving. It could be breaking loose like crazy just below the surface. You may only be moments away from seeing it fly up and be cast into the sea (Mark 11:23,24).

Avoid fainting and you're home free! So, where does fainting start? As we see in Hebrews 12:3, in your mind:

> **For consider him that endured such contradiction of sinners against himself, <u>lest ye be wearied and faint in your minds</u>.**

If you're going to get weary and faint, thereby failing to receive your due season of harvest, it's going to start in your mind—the battleground of faith.

Satan's method is to come with suggestions. "It's not working. God doesn't care about you. You're not worthy," he'll whisper. His aim is to get you to "faint in your mind." Follow Jesus' example and defeat him with "It is written."

## Trust God's Timing

Another pitfall that many believers fall into when waiting on the promises of God is comparing their experience to that of other believers.

I remember when people used to constantly ask me when I was going to go on television with this ministry. My reply was always, "It is not my time." Others would ask, "When are you going to write a book?" Again, my consistent answer was, "It is not my time."

Then one day the Lord said, "It's your time." I immediately started getting instructions from the Holy Spirit about what to do and how.

Perhaps there are some things God has placed in your heart, yet you're not presently seeing any opportunity to fulfill them. Hang on. If you'll stay in faith, the day is coming when you'll hear, "It's time."

That is why it is so important not to operate in jealousy or envy when you see God moving in the lives of others. Learn how to rejoice with those who rejoice, because your time is coming.

When you see God moving miraculously in another's life, it's too easy to sit back and grumble, "Why them and not me?" That's pure poison. And it will kill the good work God's trying to bring about in you.

Develop a child-like trust in God's timing. He loves you and has your best interests in mind.

### Hurry Up and Wait

One of the hardest things for a Christian to do is wait for God's perfect timing after He's placed a burning vision of something in your spirit. Once God has shown you what He wants, the tendency is to run out ahead of God and mess things up.

Don't do that. If God has given you a vision—it may be a ministry, a spouse, a job, or anything else—learn to wait on God's due season.

> **And the LORD answered me, and said, Write the vision, and make it plain upon tables, that he may run that readeth it. For the vision is yet for an appointed time, but at the end it shall speak, and not lie: though it tarry, wait for it; because it will surely come, it will not tarry. (Habakkuk 2:2,3)**

Here is some great advice for any believer with a vision from God. First write it down plainly. That way you'll not get carried off into something God didn't really show you.

Then, when you start feeling impatient or weary, remember, "the vision is for an appointed time...though it tarry, wait for it; because it will surely come..."

If your vision seems to be "tarrying," don't lose heart. Wait, it will surely come in due season. You have God's Word on it.

"But Pastor Dollar, I don't know how much longer I can wait. I'm really getting tired of standing!"

That's okay. Keep standing. God has made provision for you:

> **Hast thou not known? hast thou not heard, that the everlasting God, the LORD, the Creator of the ends of the earth, fainteth not, neither is weary? there is no searching of his understanding. He giveth power to the faint; and to them that have no might he increaseth strength. Even the youths shall faint and be weary, and the young men shall utterly fall: But they that wait upon the LORD shall renew their strength; they shall mount up with wings as eagles; they shall run, and not be weary; and they shall walk, and not faint. (Isaiah 40:28:31)**

To wait on the Lord means to serve God with praise, worship and adoration as a server in a restaurant would serve or wait on a customer. If the waiter does an exceptional job of serving, the customer will be motivated to leave a tip.

Child of God, I believe that when we serve God with praise and worship, God is motivated to tip us generously by causing the unrealities of our lives to become realties.

If you are in need of healing, wait on the Lord. If you are in need of a miracle, wait on the Lord. If you've grown weary from standing, wait on the Lord. If you are in need of strength, wait on the Lord. If you're feeling faint, wait on the Lord. It's a guaranteed prescription for gaining the reality of God's Word and renewed strength.

It is also the vital ninth step in God's divine order of faith.

# Chapter 12
# Step Ten: Expect the Answer

**For surely there is an end; and thine expectation shall not be cut off. (Proverbs 23:18)**

We've now come to the final step in God's established order for getting from any challenge or crisis to a miraculous solution. It is the icing on the cake...the last nail in the devil's coffin. This important tenth step involves cultivating expectation.

Expectation is a very powerful thing. For better or for worse, it colors your outlook, shapes your attitudes and influences your actions. And learning to harness its power can make a huge difference in your quality of life.

### Expectation Defined

To expect means "to wait on, anticipate, or look for something to happen." When you "expect" something, you start mentally or visually "looking" for its appearance.

For example, when your aunt says, "I'm frying chicken tonight. Come on over and have dinner with us," you expect to eat fried chicken when you get there. You are looking for it to be on the table when you arrive.

If you show up only to find meat loaf on the table, you're shocked. Why? Because you expected chicken.

Expectation not only involves a change of vision (you're now looking for something), it also involves a change of posture (you start preparing for something). When you expect something, you begin to suitably position yourself to receive it. Let me illustrate.

When a woman is with child, we say she is...what? Expecting. What is she expecting? A baby! And that expectation triggers a lot of preparation.

Furniture is purchased. A nursery is decorated. A hospital is chosen and financial arrangements are made.

Every part of that household begins to realign itself in anticipation of the expected arrival.

What would you think if you asked a woman who was going to deliver twins in a month if she was getting ready for the arrival of the babies, and she said, "No, we're not making any preparations." You'd be dumbfounded. Why? Because expectation implies preparation.

As we're about to see, this is especially true of spiritual expectation. If you are truly expecting God to do some things in your life, you will do some realigning and preparing.

I liken it to the exchange between a pitcher and a catcher in baseball. You'll never see a good catcher nonchalantly standing behind the plate waiting for the next pitch. No, when he's ready to receive, he'll crouch down, get a wide, stable base with his legs, hold up his catcher's mitt and look right at the pitcher in intense anticipation of the next pitch.

That is how the pitcher knows the catcher's ready to receive. He has put himself in the receiving posture. That pitcher is not about to throw the ball until he sees that posture.

The same is true of God. His heart-felt desire is to throw blessings to you. He's ready to wind up and let healing, prosperity and deliverance fly, but he can't until you get into a receiving posture—the posture of expectation.

I've spoken with many Christians who are "hoping and praying" for miracles, yet their posture says they're not ready to receive. Why? They don't really expect an answer. They lack genuine expectation.

### Focusing Your Expectation

The Bible has a lot to say about expectation. Let's look as Psalm 62:5,6 for starters:

**My soul, wait thou only upon God; for my expectation is from him. He only is my rock and my sal-**

**vation: he is my defence; I shall not be moved.**

Notice the focus of the psalmist's expectation, "...my expectation is from him [God]." That highlights one of the biggest problems Christians have in the area of expectation. Improper focus.

Some believers talk a good, religious talk, but when it comes right down to it, their expectation is not directed toward God. Some are expecting the world and the world's system to deliver the things that make for happiness. Others expect a relationship to meet their needs. Still others look to their pastor to spoon-feed them and do all their praying for them.

In each case, the person's expectation is focused on something or someone other than God. Yet the psalmist said, "My soul, wait thou only upon God." He's commanding his soul (his mind, will, and emotions) to get its focus off of anything but God.

Properly focused expectation says, "I'm not looking for help from any source but God. If I'm going to have it, it's going to have to come from Him. If it doesn't come from Him, I don't need it."

### The Hope Connection

Real, Bible expectation often travels with a companion. Her name is "Hope." You see them hanging out together in Philippians 1:20:

> **According to my earnest expectation and my hope, that in nothing I shall be ashamed, but that with all boldness, as always, so now also Christ shall be magnified in my body, whether it be by life, or by death.**

Hope and earnest expectation complement each other perfectly. They also tend to intensify each other. Hope increases your level of expectation—an increase in your expectation level raises your hopes. Here's how.

Let's say you have a bill you just don't have the money to pay. But because you have heard several testimonies of people who's bills have been miraculously paid, you have a little hope that God will meet your need as well. So, you pray and ask God to take care of your bill.

At that point you have a little bit of hope and fairly low level of expectation. But as you stand on God's Word and meditate the appropriate scriptures, your need is miraculously met.

The next time you are faced with a bill you can't pay, you are going to have a larger measure of hope and a higher level of expectation. This cycle repeats itself each time you experience the faithfulness of God and the effectiveness of His Word. It's an upward spiral of ever increasing hope and expectancy.

This works in the negative, too. If you throw up a half-hearted prayer and never open your Bible, you're probably not going to see an answer to your prayer. When nothing happens you'll say, "Just as I expected. Faith didn't work for me." You've developed a negative expectation and are locked in hopelessness.

### Cultivating Expectation

If you really want to receive everything from God he so greatly desires to give you, you must begin to cultivate expectancy. A number of biblical examples illustrate how important expectations are when it comes to receiving a miracle.

Remember the four men in Luke 5:17 who lowered the lame man to Jesus through a hole in the ceiling? Do you recall the first thing Jesus said to the man?

> **And when he saw their faith, he said unto him, Man, thy sins are forgiven thee. (Luke 5:20)**

This man needed healing, yet Jesus told him his sins were forgiven. Why? Jesus knew that if the man was going to receive his healing, he needed to increase his expectancy. And as we have seen, that requires a change of posture.

The man apparently had a sinful past and as a result didn't feel worthy to be healed by Jesus. Before the man would receive, Jesus had to change his expectation and that meant dealing with his sense of sinfulness.

A high level of expectancy is almost always a prerequisite for a miracle. The good news is that Jesus—as He did with the man in this passage—is always looking for a way to help us raise our level of expectation.

When a crippled man in Jerusalem needed that kind of help one day, the Holy Spirit showed Peter how to give it to him:

> **Now Peter and John went up together into the temple at the hour of prayer, being the ninth hour. And a certain man lame from his mother's womb was carried, whom they laid daily at the gate of the temple which is called Beautiful... (Acts 3:1-2)**

Here is a man who had been crippled all his life. Begging is all he'd ever known. He certainly had no reason to "expect" to ever walk or work.

Apparently, the man kept his eyes on the ground in humility and shame as he begged for alms. Yet Peter, sensing the man needed a change in posture in order to receive, gave him a command:

> **And Peter, fastening his eyes upon him with John, said, Look on us. And he gave heed unto them, expecting to receive something of them. (Acts 3:4-5)**

Peter's demand obviously had its intended effect. The man looked up at them in anticipation of receiving money. He now had expectation, but the wrong one. So Peter raised it another notch:

> **Then Peter said, Silver and gold have I none; but such as I have give I thee: In the name of Jesus Christ of Nazareth rise up and walk. And he took him by the right hand, and lifted him up:**

Peter said, "Don't expect money. Expect healing." And then to help him change his receiving posture even further, Peter grabbed him by the hand and pulled him to his feet. The result?

...and immediately his feet and ankle bones received strength. And he leaping up stood, and walked, and entered with them into the temple, walking, and leaping, and praising God. (Acts 3:7-8)

Child of God, I can't overemphasize the importance of earnest expectation in receiving the provision of God. It can turn your road to a miracle from a treacherous mountain trail into a four lane highway. There is something about expectation that places you before the face of God. God blesses expectant people.

Cultivate expectancy in every area of your life. Don't just throw your tithe into the plate and forget about it. Spend the rest of the week in earnest expectation of the windows of heaven opening up and pouring out a blessing. Expect to receive a hundred-fold return on all your giving. Expect to walk in health and to be healed when you don't. Expect to be promoted. Expect to have a good marriage.

Expect ALL the blessings of God to be yours in fullness here and now. It's what He wants for you. He says so in Jeremiah 29:11:

**For I know the thoughts that I think toward you, saith the LORD, thoughts of peace, and not of evil, to give you an expected end.**

God's desires for you are for peace, prosperity and for an expected end. In other words, "Don't let go of your earnest expectation. It will come in the end."

When you pray according to God's Word, expect an answer. It's the tenth and final step in God's divine order of faith.

### The Road to Your Answer

There they are—ten simple, Bible-based steps that will take you to victory over any problem you may ever face.

1. Identify the Problem
2. Make a Quality Decision to Overcome the Problem God's Way
3. Find Your Title Deed to an Answer in God's Word
4. Hear the Word Concerning Your Victory
5. Meditate the Word to Plant it in Your Heart
6. Confess the Word to Release Your Faith
7. Act on the Word
8. Apply the Pressure of Patience
9. Understand there is an Appointed Time and Due Season
10. Expect the Answer

These steps represent God's established order for successfully operating in faith. And as we've seen over and over, divine order is a prerequisite for miracles.

You never have to experience another "faith failure" as long as you live. You never again have to feel the frustration of not being able to get faith to work for you as it does for others. You are now prepared to walk in all of the abundant life Jesus died to purchase for you. You now can be free.

All this is true because you understand God's divine order of faith.